D1759355

SNAKE

LIFE CYCLES

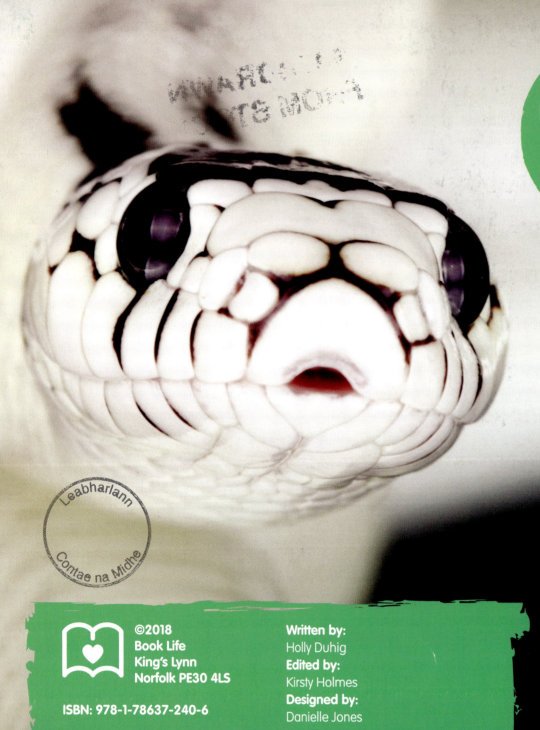

Words that look like **this** can be found in the glossary on page 24.

©2018
Book Life
King's Lynn
Norfolk PE30 4LS

ISBN: 978-1-78637-240-6

Written by:
Holly Duhig
Edited by:
Kirsty Holmes
Designed by:
Danielle Jones

A catalogue record for this book
is available from the British Library.

SNAKE

LIFE CYCLES

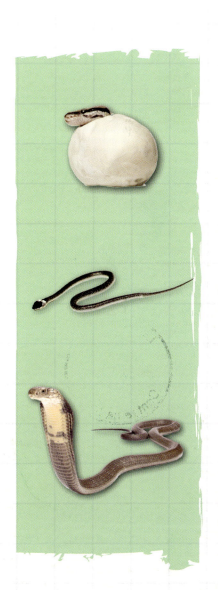

WHAT IS A LIFE CYCLE?

All animals, plants and humans go through different stages of their life as they grow and change. This is called a life cycle.

Human Life Cycle

Baby → Child → Adult

WHAT IS A SNAKE?

A snake is a **reptile**. Snakes have long, scaly bodies with no arms or legs. Different species of snake have skins of different colours.

Some snake bites can kill or seriously harm!

EGGS

Female snakes lay eggs. Snake eggs are a similar size to chicken eggs but they are white and feel rubbery to touch.

Some species of snake lay only a few eggs. Others lay up to 100!

Snakes look for somewhere dark and safe to lay their eggs, such as **hollow** logs or dips in the ground. This keeps the eggs hidden from **predators**.

It is important that the eggs are safe because most snake parents don't stay to protect them.

SNAKELETS

Baby snakes are called snakelets. Snakelets break out of their egg using a special egg tooth. They lose this tooth once they've hatched.

When snakelets first hatch, they look like adult snakes but much smaller and much thinner. They eat small animals, like mice or rats.

Snakelets that have just hatched are called hatchlings.

GROWING SNAKELETS

Snakelets usually moult about four times a year.

As snakelets grow, they 'moult'. This means they shed their skin and grow a new one. Snakes need to moult as they grow otherwise their skin gets too tight.

Snakelets are often born with the same amount of **venom** as an adult snake. This is because they have to be able to protect themselves.

SNAKES

Snakelets become adult snakes when they are fully grown.
Adult snakes spend their time looking for a **mate** so they
can lay eggs of their own.

Green anaconda snakes live in swamps and rivers. Their skin colour keeps them **camouflaged** in the water, where they lie in wait for their **prey**.

Green Anaconda

Scarlet king snakes and coral snakes look very similar but telling the difference is very important. One is harmless and one is venomous.

People have made up a clever rhyme to remember which snake is dangerous. 'Red touching yellow kills a fellow. Red touching black – friend of Jack.'

Venomous Coral Snake

SCARY SNAKES

Tiger Keelback

The tiger keelback snake steals **poison** from its prey! They eat poisonous frogs and store up the poison to use for themselves.

16

Did you know that some snakes can fly? The flying snake **glides** from tree-to-tree by flattening its body and flinging itself off branches.

Flying Snake

Flying snakes flatten to an 's' shape to glide on the air.

LOOKING FOR FOOD

Boa Constrictor

Adult snakes spend most of their time hunting. Some snakes wrap themselves around their prey and squeeze tight. Others have a venomous bite.

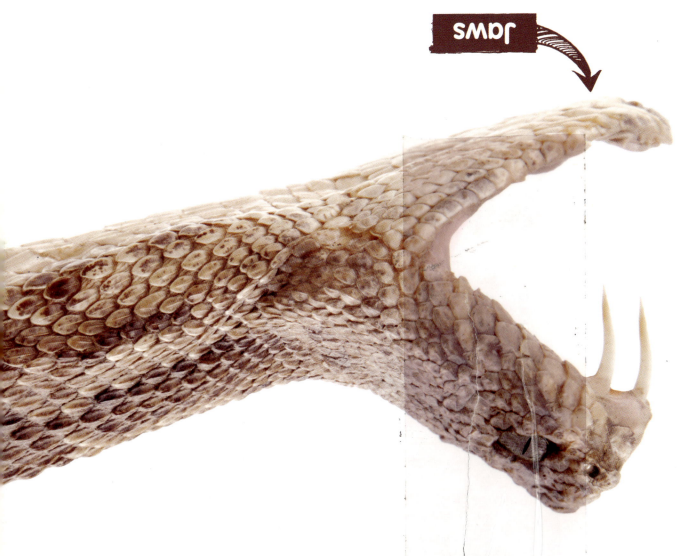

Jaws

Snakes have **jaws** which stretch like elastic bands and allow them to swallow animals whole. Snakes have been known to swallow animals as big as pigs and antelopes!

Medusa the Python

WORLD RECORD BREAKERS

World's Longest Snake in Captivity

The record for the longest snake kept in **captivity** is held by Medusa, a python who is 7.67 metres long! She weighs a massive 158.8 kilograms.

⭐ World's Longest Snake Fangs ⭐

A species of snake called the Gaboon viper holds the record for the longest fangs. The viper's fangs can grow up to five centimetres long!

LIFE CYCLE OF A SNAKE

LIFE CYCLES

1
A female snake lays her eggs in a safe place.

2
Snakelets bite their way out of their eggs using their egg tooth.

3
Snakelets moult many times as they become adult snakes.

4
Adult snakes look for a mate so they can lay eggs of their own.

GET EXPLORING!

What else can you find out about snakes? Many zoos have a reptile house where you can go and see snakes and find out more about them.

GLOSSARY

camouflaged	when an animal is hard to see because it is the same colour as its habitat
captivity	being kept and looked after by humans
glide	to move in a smooth continuous motion
hollow	having a hole or empty space in the middle
jaws	the upper and lower part of the mouth containing the teeth
mate	a partner (of the same species) who an animal chooses to produce young with
poison	a substance which is dangerous or deadly
predators	animals that hunt other animals for food
prey	animals that are hunted by other animals for food
reptile	a cold–blooded animal with scales
venom	a harmful substance that is injected through a bite or a sting

INDEX

PHOTO CREDITS

Photocredits: Abbreviations: l-left, r-right, b-bottom, t-top, c-centre, m-middle.
Front Cover —jeep2499. 1 – jeep2499. 2 – trangk. 3t – Eric Isselee, 3m – Bignai, 3b – reptiles4all.
4l – Oksana Kuzmina, 4m – studioloco, 4r – Ljupco Smokovski. 5 – PetlinDmitry. 6 – Eric Isselee. 7 – Noppharat616. 8 – bluedog studio.
9 – Heiko Kiera. 10 – Sakdinon Kadchiangsaen. 11 – Robert Eastman. 12 – Tenshi. 13 – Vladimir Wrangel. 14 – Patrick K. Campbell. 15 – Patrick K.
Campbell. 16 – eye-blink. 17 – george photo cm .18 – Natalia Kuzmina. 19 – Chuck Rausin. 20 – VectorShow. 21 – Brimac The 2nd [CC BY 2.0
(http://creativecommons.org/licenses/by/2.0)], via Wikimedia Commons. 22t – Noppharat616, 22l – Vanatchanan, 22b – AjayTvm, 22r – Ery Azmeer.
23 – AdaCo. Images are courtesy of Shutterstock.com. With thanks to Getty Images, Thinkstock Photo and iStockphoto.